Poems *of* Me

Stephen Perez

ISBN: 978-1-962363-55-6 (sc)
ISBN: 978-1-962363-56-3 (e)

Rev. date: 01/15/2024

Contents

I want to be the One

I want to be the one that makes you laugh.
The one that wakes up next to you.

I want to be the one that drives you crazy,
The one that takes care of you.

I want to be the one that spends his life with you.
The one that's always on your mind.

I want to be the one that you call when you're in
trouble, Whenever you find yourself in a bind.

I want to be the one that makes your eyes
sparkle, The one that makes your life complete.

I want to be the one that turns your world upside
down, The one that makes your life so sweet.

When I Look at You

When I look at you, I see an angel.
Someone that will make my life so special.

Someone that will turn my world upside
down, Where hugs and kisses will abound.

When I look at you, I see someone
that can make my life a dream.
Someone that will always be my queen.

When I look at you, I see a person that I want in my
life, A person that I hope will someday be my wife.

When You Know You're in Love

When she's all you think about,
You can't get her off your mind,
When you want to be around her
All of the time.

When you're talking to your friends
And she keeps coming up,
When you look at her
And you can't get enough.

When you're around her and you
Find it hard to breathe,
You start to sweat
And your heart skips a beat.

When you look at her
and you can't imagine your life without her,
You can't wait to be with her tomorrow.

What Could Have Been

We met by chance, or was it?
Our hearts seemed like they
already knew each other.
Could they have been together in another time?
The feeling is strong, why fight it? Why bother?

Although you said that you want nothing serious,
You gave me a chance anyway.
Me, like a love-sick teenager,
Thought that I could change your mind,

We spent time together,
And I fell deeply in love.
My life as I knew it began to unwind.

As time went on,
I would come to ask you to spend your life with me.
To me, the time we spent together,
was time well spent.

You said that you couldn't because
you were not ready.
I suspect that you were scared,
Hurt as I was, I had to accept it.
I guess we will never know what could have been.

The Storm

It came in one late August night.
They called it Harvey, and it gave us quite a fright,
It left behind a path of destruction,
Like many had not seen before.
It took out trees and power and so much more.

It only lasted a few hours, and then it was gone.
From the one's who stayed and survived,
Came the saying "Texas Strong,"

Although it dampened our spirits,
and knocked us down,
We were bound and determined, out
of this we would rebound.

It will take more than a little storm
To make us Texans go away,
We are here for the long haul, we are here to stay.

You might not be from Texas And
therefore, think you don't belong,
If you have courage, compassion,
and determination, You can consider
yourself, "Texas Strong."

NFL's 2017, Man of the Year

They named him "The Man of the Year."
But he is more than that,
He plays football for the Houston
Texans, And his name is J.J. Watt.

When Hurricane Harvey came knocking,
J.J. answered the door.
He distributed supplies and did a whole lot more.

He raised a lot of money for the relief
effort, And asked for nothing in return,
There are lessons here
For the whole world to learn.

He is a man of integrity,
And a giant among his peers,
He affected a lot of lives,
So, yes, he deserves to be "Man of the Year."

Dad

He was your first hero, He's as tall as the sky,
He can do anything; He's the best in your eyes.

He's the one you call when you get hurt,
He will wipe your tears away whenever you cry,

He provides you with everything you need;
He keeps you in line,

Whenever you need him,
He'll be there every time.

He does not always get the recognition he deserves,
Often times, he's left out.

He does not complain-taking care of his
family, That's what he's all about.

I'll Never Know

Dedicated to my daughter, Yvette Marie Perez
5/22/05-5/25/05

I'll never know the sound of your little cries,
Waking up at 2. AM because you're hungry.

I'll never now the sound of your little voice,
When you get hurt and cry out for Daddy.

I'll never get to hold your hand as I
walk you to school, Wipe your tears
away, as you cry on that first day,

I'll never get to hear your laughter,
Whenever you watch cartoons on Saturday,

I'll never know what a beautiful young
lady, You would have grown up to be,

I'll never know why you had to go,
Why you were taken from me.

They say that time heals a broken
heart, And everything gets better.

I don't know the truth in that,
I miss you more and more every
day, My angel, my daughter.

My Love

My love, if I had traveled the world looking
for someone to give my heart to..
I still could never find anyone as special as you.

As we get our lives started together,
Let our hearts beat as one.
Our future together looks as bright
as the noon day sun.

You make me happy, you brighten my life, My
hope is that one day you will be my wife.

The Twinkle in Your Eye

As you both start your lives together,
Work to keep the gleam in your eye,

That spark that first lit up when you met,
That feeling that gave you your romantic high.

As you travel down the road of
life, keep that fire burning,
It will keep your future bright and
give you a better tomorrow,

If the road gets a little bumpy and things look dark,
Just cling to each other and you
will never know sorrow,

Many things in the world can get you down,
But the love in your heart is as deep as the ocean,

As long as you have that twinkle in your
eye, True love can never be broken.

Letter to my First Grandson

In every life there is one person
you cannot live without.

In my life, you are the one.
I cannot imagine my life without you in it.

You are the light of my life, the one
person that keeps me going.

To say that I love you would not even
begin to say how I feel about you.

I never knew I could love someone so much,
Everything I am, and everything
I do is because of you.

I can't wait to see what kind of young man
you will grow to be.

I am so proud of you.

Love,
PawPaw

Angel on the Ground
Dedicated to my friend Krystle Keller

You were a beacon of light in my darkest hour,
you will never know what you did for me.

At a time when I was really down on myself,
you made me see who I could be.

You made me feel good about myself, you
really pumped up my self-esteem.

You made me feel so much pride,
I was bursting at the seam.

You gave me Confidence,
you made me feel ten feet tall.

I'll never forget you,
you were my shining angel.

A Mother's Love

A mother's love is unconditional and unwavering,
she will always be there when you need her.

A mother's love is everlasting,
there is no other love that can compare.

A mother's love can see you through your darkest
hour, when you get your heart broken or you
lose your best friend.

A Mother's love is the strongest bond you will ever
know, no other love in your life will be as true.

A mother's love will be there even when
times are bad, she might not always like
you, but she will always love you!

Road to Nowhere

I started off on my vacation trip.
I noticed the streets were empty,
I could sense there was something in the air.
I'm on the road to nowhere.

I get to where I planned to go,
and look for a motel.
I find one and go in to ask for a room,
and I get an empty stare.
I'm on the road to nowhere.

I want something to eat,
so I look for a restaurant.
I drive around for a while,
and can't find one open anywhere.
I'm on the road to nowhere.

So if you hit the road for a little adventure,
you might want to call ahead.
Be sure you have time to spare,
you might find yourself
on the road to nowhere.

Mother

M is for the many nights she stayed up
  taking care of you when you were ill.

O is for overworked- having a 9 to 5 and still
  taking care of the house and family.

T is for the tireless hours she puts in to
  make sure everything runs smoothly.

H is for the Home she makes out of the
          dwelling that you live in.

E is for all the Extra hours she puts in at home,
    her day is 30 hrs. instead of 24.

R is for Regrets of which she has none,
      she would do it all over again.

Thank you mom.